LULU the Tiger
Loves Ice Cream

by ANN LEE

Lulu the Tiger opens a letter from Hal Hippo.
She's super excited –
she stands on her tigertastic tiptoes.

"I know just the dessert to bring,"
Lulu sings.

"I'll make some ice cream,
the yummiest of things,"

Lulu decides to make her
three favorite flavors:
Vanilla, chocolate and strawberry
for everyone to savor.

Lulu gathers the ingredients for her tasty ice cream.

Milk, honey, vanilla, chocolate, strawberries, and cream – what a dream!

In three bowls, Lulu pours
the milk, cream, and honey,
Then adds vanilla, chocolate, and
strawberries and pats her tummy!
Lulu stirs, blends, and mixes each one.
Making ice cream is so much fun!

Lulu pours the ice cream into
a container with ease.
Now it's time for the ice cream to freeze.

Lulu adds the container
in the freezer to set.
She waits and waits –
is the ice cream ready yet?

Lulu waits a couple of hours.
And while she waits, she waters the flowers.

The delicious ice cream is finally ready. She opens the door and says goodbye to her teddy.

Lulu arrives at the party,
and oh what a sight!
She spots a long table
full of sweets and delights.

Lulu puts hers on the table,
quick as a fox,
Then runs to her friends
playing in the sandbox.

Gregory Giraffe glides down a slippery slide.
Penelope Parrot spies a carousel and goes for a ride.
Eddy Elephant looks for hidden treasures by the trees.

Everyone is enjoying the fun and games.
"It's time for dessert," Hal Hippo exclaims.

The friends all gather round to taste –
No dessert can go to waste.

They try Hal Hippo's muffins topped with cherries.
They gobble up Zoe Zebra's cupcakes filled with berries.

They pick at Gregory Giraffe's smash cake, which looks kind of runny.
They nibble on Penelope Parrot's cookies covered in ooey, gooey honey.
And they eat Eddy Elephant's waffles, which taste a bit funny.

Lulu giggles and teases, "No, it's something better.
But if you leave it in the sun, it'll only get wetter."

Lulu Tiger grins and declares, "Ice cream is my favorite treat. Chocolate, strawberry, vanilla, or anything sweet,

Helps to beat summer's sizzling heat.
And look, I can do a fantastic trick."
She opens the lid with a sudden flick.

Lulu tosses the scoops up into the air.
And catches them in a cone with
fantastic flair.

All the friends laugh and cheer.
But one scoop falls to the ground,
oh dear!

Everyone has a scoop,
except for Gregory Giraffe.
But Lulu has an idea and
snorts a tiger laugh.

"Let's share our scoops and
try all the flavors.
This is what I call a friendship favor."
The friends agree and
soon all the ice cream is eaten.
It's the favorite party dessert
that can't be beaten.

"We have a winning dessert," Hal Hippo rings a bell.

All the friends agree and yell:
"I scream, you scream,
We all scream for LULU's ice cream!"

Enjoyed your copy of
LULU the Tiger
Loves Ice Cream?

Please find the next part of LULU the Tiger Cooking Adventures;

LULU the Tiger and the Yummiest Pizza

on Amazon.com

Special GIFT for you.
LULU's Color book can be
downloaded here;
https://BookHip.com/ZRJCVD

LULU THE TIGER
LOVES ICE
CREAM

RECIPE

Want a free book?

Please get your copy of
The Best Color of All at:

https://BookHip.com/KJSCBR

About author

Ann Lee is an author and mother. Her children are the joy of her life and the inspiration for her writing. She decided early on that learning how to cook was not only an excellent way to stay healthy, but fundamental for her children as they grow up.

Lulu the Tiger Loves Ice Cream, is her third book in the Cooking Adventures series, where she combines her imagination with teaching children how to cook.

More information about Ann and her books can be found at luluthetiger.com.

Printed in Great Britain
by Amazon

79867361R00025